STARLIGHT

Written by JULIA ARTIS

Illustrated by JUWI JAKASHI

First published in 2023
Published by Journey Together Publishing

Written by Julia Artis
Illustrated by Fuuji Takashi
Book design by Bryony van der Merwe

ISBN: 979-8-3507-0600-0 (hardcover)
ISBN: 979-8-218-13690-1 (paperback)
ISBN: 979-8-218-17134-6 (ebook)

Dedicated to

my HUSBAND Ron Artis II

and the child within
each and everyone's heart.

Once there
was a **little STAR.**
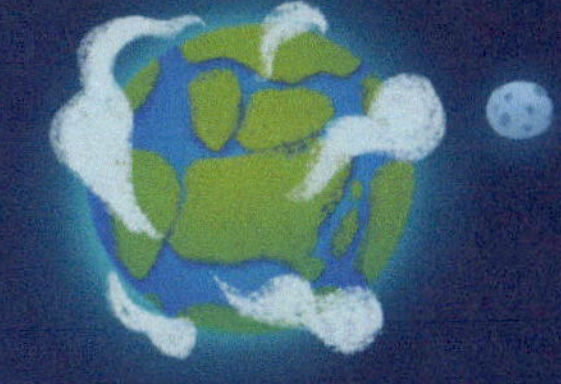

Shining bright
and oh so far.

But suddenly he
lost his LIGHT.
and felt LONELY
in the night.

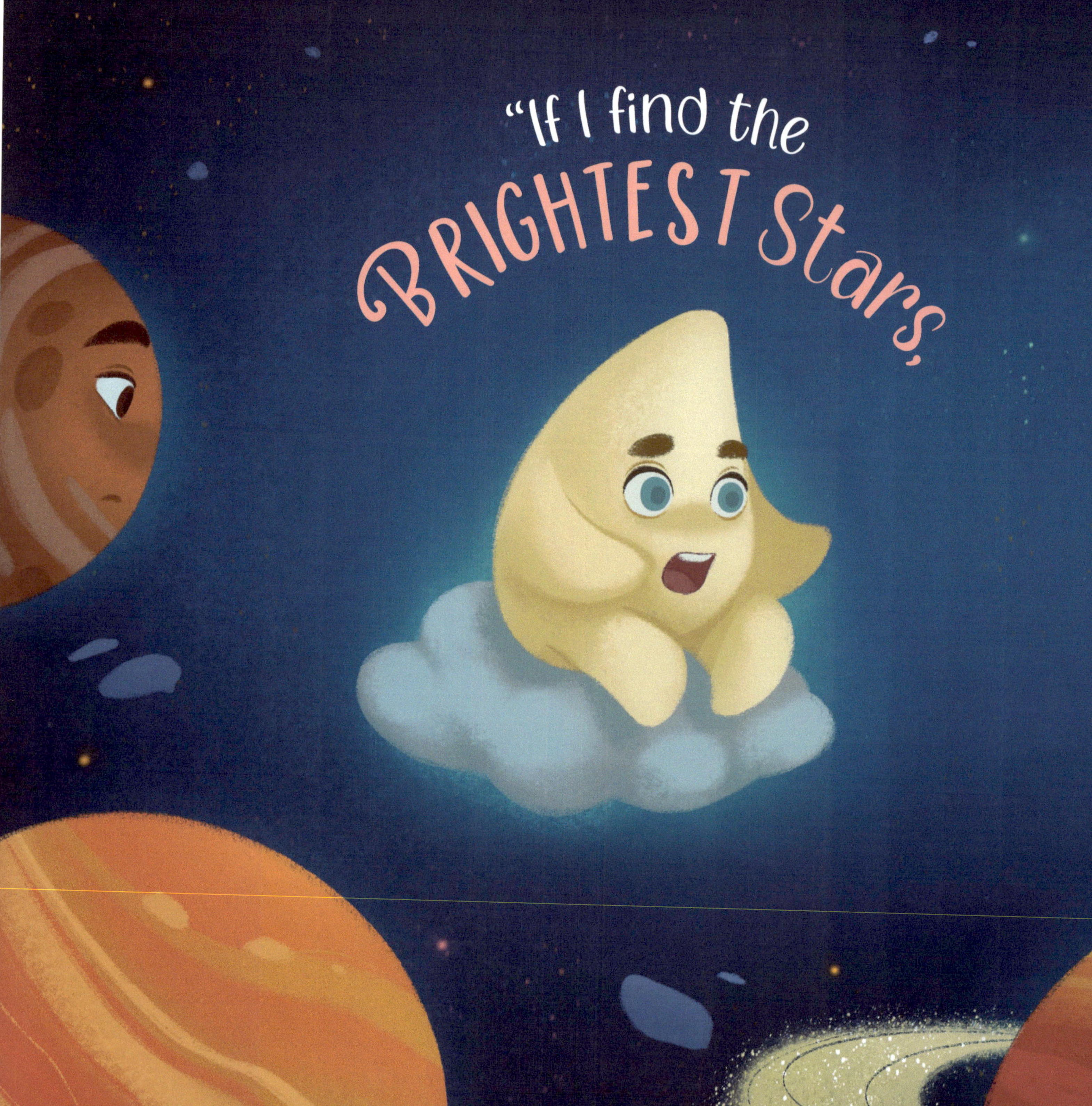

"If I find the
BRIGHTEST Stars,

I'll SHINE
like them!"
he said
to Mars.

But the
BRIGHT ones
didn't help
him much. .

HERO OF THE GALAXY
Amongst them
he felt LIKE A
SMUDGE.

He journeyed on
to the
palace of LIGHT.

To gain
the glow in
mindful SIGHT.

He studied to be
SMART
and bright

but stayed
INVISIBLE
at night.

On he flew
to the LAST one
that could help.

The man of
SUCCESS,
where money
prevailed.

He worked for
endless hours
and DAYS,

collected
coins and
shiny WAYS.

Still,
his heart stayed
heavy
and GREY.

He missed his
glow and
HAPPY
days.

When he was
ready to

give UP
and fall,
he realized
that's what
it was,

after ALL.

"God please grant me the **STRENGTH** to be me. And I shall be **FAITHFUL** and **SHINE** for thee."

A big STORM grabbed him and whirled him around.

He felt he'd been caught
by the peace he had found.

Before he knew it
he was HOME
after all,

shining
brighter
than ever

straight from his SOUL.

About the AUTHOR

This former federal criminal detective.
World traveling mother of 5.
Has lived a life full of adversity, triumph,
beauty and perseverance.
Born Nov. 28th 1983 in East Germany behind the wall.
With dreams of one day freely seeing the world.

She would later graduate with an MBA, start her career at the
BKA (Bundeskriminalamt). Then in 2010, she resigned and traveled
the world. Later moving to Hawaii in 2012, and starting a family.
She likes to say "Have the courage to listen to God".
Only he knows your true purpose.